MW01227091

DragonFly
Unleashed

Marcia Marie Moore

ISBN: 9798398894677

DEDICATION

This book is dedicated to my Lord and Savior Jesus Christ, my family, friends and
life's lessons to birth out what was necessary for a time such as now.
DragonFly Unleashed has been in the making for a few years but
God's timing is never late.
Be healed, inspired, ignited and transformed to be all who you were created to be!

TABLE OF CONTENTS

Introduction

DragonFly Unleashed is a combination of realistic short stories, scenarios and poetry that can be relatable to many. Learning to break free from the molds one is shaped in and embracing all who you were created to be is liberating. Life lessons of self-discovery, self-love, spiritual awakening, love, loss, acceptance and hope make for an intriguing ride of awareness and connection. Enjoy my journey through each page as you gain hope, wisdom and revelation for your future. Don't forget to pick a favorite or two to re-read often for more insight, understanding and healing.

D.O.P.E.

DYNAMIC deep soul bringing messages of light via DragonFly;

OPTIMAL in thought, action and deed, always on a natural high.

PANACEAL through health and wellness offering a solution or remedy for all difficulties and disease;

EMPATHETIC displaying God's love for mankind's peace.

D.O.P.E.

I am a dope individual, a rare blend of creativity, wisdom, and compassion. My soul runs deep, a wellspring of insight that bubbles to the surface in the form of poetry and profound thought. With every word, I strive to bring messages of light, illuminating the darkest corners of the world and offering hope to those who need it most.

In thought, action, and deed, I am always seeking to elevate my mind, body, and spirit. I live my life on a natural high from God's presence, fueled by the boundless energy that comes from aligning with my purpose and passions. My zest for life is infectious, inspiring those around me to strive for greatness and embrace the power within themselves.

As a beacon of health and wellness, I offer solutions and remedies for life's difficulties and diseases. My knowledge and expertise in well-being extend beyond the physical, nurturing emotional and spiritual health as well. With every breath, I embody the healing power of God's natural ways, helping others to find balance and harmony in their lives.

But perhaps my most potent gift is my empathy, a divine reflection of God's love for humanity. Through my understanding and compassion, I offer solace and support to those in need, fostering peace and unity among mankind. I walk this earth with purpose and grace, leaving a trail of inspiration and hope in my wake. My heart overflows with kindness, and I am dedicated to spreading love and light wherever I go.

IN AWE OF YOU

It was a time in my life when I felt like I had hit rock bottom. I had been struggling with various personal and professional challenges, and it seemed like nothing was going my way. In the depths of my despair, I turned to God, praying for guidance and relief from my troubles. Little did I know that my prayers were about to be answered in the most extraordinary way.

I stumbled upon an opportunity that seemed too good to be true but it was real. This new season not only provided me with inner peace and stability but also reignited my passion for purpose.

My life was now filled with love, laughter, and support, making every day feel like a blessing. This sense of purpose and fulfillment made me realize that God was truly working in my life, giving me everything I had prayed for and more.

From that moment on, I felt incredibly blessed. My faith in God's plan for me had been restored, and I knew that I was meant to do great things. I was grateful for the challenges I had faced, as they helped me grow into the person I was meant to become. And as I continued to walk the path laid out before me, I was filled with an overwhelming sense of gratitude for the countless blessings God had bestowed upon my life.

In Awe of You

Never would I have imagined the top of this mountain.

Anticipating my needs and cater to my existence.

It is true that God will give you more than you could ever hope for or imagine.

The love is so overwhelming that I can barely gasp a breath before the next blessing

comes down the lane like 10 striked pins after the turkey dance on the screen.

You feel me?

First name Grace, middle name Mercy and last name, Favor

have become my new John Hancock signed on the dotted lines of every page

of this new chapter and I am loving it...restoration looks good on me.

.

SCALED

I remember the night I met him. It was a warm, clear evening when the stars seemed to be shining brighter than ever.

I was out celebrating with my friends, enjoying the ambiance of good music and laughter. As I swayed to the reggae rhythm, I noticed a guy across the dance floor, his eyes locked onto mine. It was as if fate had brought us together under that starlit sky.

He approached me, and our conversation flowed effortlessly. We laughed, shared stories, and danced the night away. The connection felt so strong, so genuine, that I couldn't help but believe he was the one. He even called me his Mrs the first night we stayed together. I couldn't tell if it was the liquor or our strong intimate connection fully clothed. For weeks, we spent every moment we could together, delving deeper into each other's lives. It felt like God was finally going to grant me the love and compatibility I had been searching for.

But as time passed, I began to notice a change in him. He grew distant, less available, and his once-warm gaze turned cold. My heart ached as I realized that he wasn't ready for the love I had to offer. I had given him my heart, my mind and my body, but he simply wasn't prepared to receive it.

Despite the pain, I learned a valuable lesson about love. Sometimes, even the most enchanting beginnings won't guarantee a fairy tale ending. But I'll always cherish that unforgettable night under the stars when I truly believed that I had found the one so here's to scales of love...

Scaled

Do you ever just want to love someone to healing?
More than just potential that you see, looking at a caged bird that needs to break free.

Stuck in a dimension of time from a crime he may or may not have even committed. But now he's on trial with a life sentence, in his mind, when he really can be acquitted.

He knows the Master judge but for whatever reason won't allow Him to advocate through the pieces of his heart, bruised soul and broken body while the mind stays on overload trying to balance the monster inside.

I know you want that beast calmed like the dead sea. But you keep surfing in oceans where the tide is too high and the thought of drowning keeps you on shore away from reaching the ultimate wave to whisk you back to the land you seek...the land of safety...peace...tranquility...strength...encouragement...exhortation and unconditional love.

To love you through your unlovable moments and to remind you that you're more than what you believe sometimes while helping you lift back up your crown when it starts to slip. Real rap, from the grip I felt the need to love on you.

To love you with that kind of MooreLove that comforts, covers, and keeps. That love that reminds you that you are that quality, unique masterpiece of art I enjoy as my premium personal collection.

Giving you that non-judgemental kind of love but not let you wallow in your mess type of love so you can edify your highest self type of love.

That 528Hz frequency type love, that restores every bad signal and crossed line so you can flow in a groove that you can chill in and vibe with for a lifetime.

But if mi neva get di chance to wine a likkle dance with you under the stars again,
just know that I pray through them stars straight to the throne for you to heal in every way so you can love and be loved again the right way.

With that restorative type of love, that can only come from God as your Source.
That transformative type of love that brings out all who you were created to be and sets you on course.

That Agape type love that reminds you He created you marvelously complex
so learn to love all of you as He does...because He is pleased in what He created in life's vortex.

Mannnn... if I could only get you to see what I see and know what I know...to trust Love one more time...
I promise you it's different with growth...

TIED SOULS

When I first met him, I was instantly drawn to his magnetic energy and captivating presence. The connection between us felt so powerful and all-consuming that I believed we were destined to be together. We were a breath of fresh air for each other. I thought our relationship was built on a growing love, a deep and undeniable bond that would withstand the test of time.

As the days turned into months, it became increasingly clear that something was amiss. The intense emotions that had once brought us together now seemed to be tearing us apart. We found ourselves locked in a cycle of passion and pain, our hearts entwined in a tangled web of desire and dependency.

It was then that I began to question the nature of our connection. As I dug deeper, I discovered the concept of soul ties - emotional bonds formed through intense relationships that can sometimes be more toxic than healthy. I realized that what I had mistaken for love was, in fact, a soul tie, a bond that left me feeling drained and emotionally scarred.

The revelation shook me to my core, as I struggled to come to terms with the reality of our relationship. I knew that I needed to break free from this toxic soul tie and rediscover the true meaning of love - a love based on mutual respect, trust, and genuine affection.

With a heavy heart of disappointment, yet again, I embarked on a journey of healing and self-discovery. I sought support from friends, family, and my spiritual beliefs, working to untangle the threads that had bound our souls together. With each passing day, I began to rediscover my own strength and worth, learning to stand on my own two feet once more.

Though the process was painful and challenging, I emerged from the experience with newfound clarity and understanding. I now recognize the difference between a true connection and a soul tie, and I am better equipped to navigate the complexities of relationships.

The relationship that I once believed was rooted in love served as a valuable lesson, teaching me the importance of self-awareness and the power of genuine love to heal and uplift. Though the soul tie has been severed, the wisdom I gained from the experience will remain with me always.

Tied Souls

It was the look in your eye, that swag that style,
Firm but gentle, hadn't felt that in a while.
As the breeze blows and the music flows enjoying swapped energies anticipating the unknown...
His touch, my touch wasn't expecting too much yet souls intertwined by stimulating convos under the cosmos
that neither wanted to end.

Where have I been all these years you ask?
Waiting for you to be ready for me to make many more years transcend...but...this time with healed hearts and
lust turn to longing as the comfort and ease between our beings destined for a time such as now...

They say air and water don't mix
but I always need restoration from a beach day fix.
The perfect combo of a breeze flowing through me as the waves crash around me is perfect harmony. Skinny
dipping in the deep end of the ocean,
damn, we done went too deep where air and water are on reserve.

I wanted what I wanted and you invited me to be free, so I opened up all of me
and when I gave it to you the experience was heavenly but whether it was too much for you,
the timing was bad for longevity
or I was just not your cup of tea
Just know it definitely has taken a toll on me.

I'm fighting daily to regain my strength as it has opened the desire and hunger for love not ready to be
manifested ...and it aches.

I'm tired of people who only want me as a conquest or to be on hold as a dream or an escape.

I gave you all of me because I wanted you to be mine
and then to happen chance that it didn't last
I needed you to remember me through distance and time.

I knew it was a gamble,
a risk I wasn't sure I should take
but I swore if it was the last time I gave of myself to anyone that I would treat it like the night before my wake

I wanted you to inhale me like I'm the last breath you will ever need

I wanted to feel your lips all ova as I taste your essence
Be the healing you need as I become your muse of inspiration for your next seed.

I Waited...

I promise you I waited as long as I could.
To love you to cherish you
 to honor you the only way that you should.
 I wanted you to be the one...

The one to help me run this kingdom to leave a legacy far greater than the pain of our past.
To change atmospheres and take over territories as lives are being touched with class.

But you weren't ready...

Decisions have momentum and It's a shame we weren't taught to love those that love on you....
instead we chase the wish list and desire those we should avoid like the flu.
They say that hope deferred makes the heart sick, so I must have rushed with you...

Encouraging love notes you'll never see, thoughtful gifts you'll never receive. I wanted you to be my forever but you told me go find it
and it's fine because I now know who I am in this journey of endeavors

But it's when your heart bleeds too bad for you to live again.
The pain of heartache and loss has you stuck and scared to open up ever again.

I want someone to capture still moments with, not for likes, only love of making memories that people only believe goes down in myths.

So now I just wait for the day that you are no longer relevant.
I often wonder do you feel me covering you as my prayers tuck you in at night,
And in the meantime my prayers will comfort you in your plight and my heart will continue to be guidance for your life hoping the day you choose to walk out of darkness into this marvelous light. ....

A LETTER TO MY SONS

I remember the weight of worry pressing down on my shoulders, a constant companion as I navigated through life. My concerns for my sons' well-being seemed to grow heavier with each passing day. In a world that appeared to be more focused on self-interest and material wealth, I couldn't help but worry about my children's future and their ability to find their place in society.

As a parent, I knew it was my responsibility to guide them, to encourage them to develop their unique talents and abilities. I was determined to help them understand that they have so much to offer the world, that they could be a solution to a problem and a blessing to society. But I couldn't shake the feeling that the odds were stacked against us.

I watched my sons grow and learn in a world of senseless violence and crabs in a barrel mentality. However, their inquisitive nature and kindness kept shining through. I marveled at their potential, but I also feared that the world might not see what we saw in them. I worried that they would be overlooked or undervalued, that their contributions to society would go unnoticed. The burden of these concerns weighed heavily on my heart.

Despite my fears, I remained steadfast in my commitment to support my children. Even after I left my ex-husband, the 2nd time, I continued to pour into them as best I could and taught them the importance of empathy, perseverance, and standing up for what is right. I encouraged them to seek out opportunities to make a difference, help those in need, and to use their skills and passions to contribute to the greater good. And with each small victory, I felt a glimmer of hope that my sons would indeed find their place in the world.

As I watched them grow into young adults, I began to see that my efforts had not been in vain. I saw them making a difference in the lives of those around him, using their unique perspectives to solve problems and bring about positive change. It was then that I realized my worries had been transformed into pride and gratitude for the incredible young men my sons had become.

Though the world may not always value who we are or what we have to offer, I remain hopeful that my sons will continue to be a beacon of light, a solution to problems, and a true blessing to society. And as I witness their journey, my once-heavy heart is now filled with hope, love, pride, and unwavering faith in God's protection and guidance as well as their abilities to make the world a better place.

A Letter to My Sons

Good morning son sons, I didn't think I was ready to write about this.
For I know love conquers all and I don't like to debate religion, politics, or topics that divide us like the abyss.

However...I'm at a loss for words at the inhumanity that continues to plague our Race, one Race, human race where we all bleed red....yet history, fear, hatred, and ignorance has us at war with one another and untimely deaths by dishonor are the only chatter being fed.

As I stay on my knees to pray... there's not one not two not three but five of you godly young men that I have to cover and wonder will your government jobs, trade and college educations, or hospital essential worker statuses be enough for the day that someone decides you are not worthy to exist in the same space as them.

That your hearts of God, strength and stature,
resilience and diligence, perseverance and kindness,
obedience and/or silence won't be valued like a gem.

Abuse of false power and authority are on continued rise;
and it's been said that history always repeats itself yet this is a never ending nightmare stained in our brains since technology's voice of demise.

But fear cannot cast out fear, and hate cannot drive out hate,
I can only pray and employ you to live out your God ordained purpose to leave a legacy of change as no man knows the day or hour of their eternal fate.

I long to see your purpose and destinies be fulfilled;
but sometimes the weight of this world pressures faith's strong arms to surrender to its match that has pinned its faith, hope and love down to the degree of chilled.

No parent should ever have to bury their child,
especially over someone else's BS or their profile.

Ty...I want you to continue to soar above and break the cycles for your kin,

Heed...I need you to embrace God's path of greatness for you regardless of mans' sin.

Nai...walk in your gifting of accountability to help heal the mind,

Lonnie...build up healing hearts like the engineer you are who creates & rebuilds things that bind.

19

And Sir...please transform hearts and souls to be on one accord;
with your debated words of wisdom and spirituality, knowing these are gifts that can only come from the Lord.

We love you, especially when the world does not,
try not to absorb its toxicity to produce rage and bitterness while you guys are casting lots.

Know...even when you and God have to walk alone, it's more than enough;
Always hold on to His everlasting truths and promises, especially when the journey gets rough.

Try not to get distracted on the whens and the hows;
Your patience, strength and perseverance are built on adversity so fuel it for your propelled greatness despite
what is going on right now.

Remember, you were born with value and purpose, your life has promise and potential as it unfolds in
accordance to God's Eternal plan;
So continue to be anchored in Him, standing tall, righteous, and protected black man!

HIDDEN GEM

For years, I struggled with feeling overlooked by men. It seemed like no matter how much effort I put into my appearance or how kind and engaging I tried to be, I was always passed over for someone else or not taken seriously. The sting of rejection and abandonment left me feeling unworthy and questioning my own value at times.

But over time, I began to realize that my worth wasn't determined by the attention or validation of others. I needed to appreciate and love myself for who I was, both inside and out. So, I embarked on a journey of self-discovery and self-love, learning to embrace my God-given unique qualities.

I recognized the beauty within me, not just in my physical appearance, but in my love and compassion for others. They were my gifts from the Almighty. I discovered my innate sense of intrigue yet the godliness that resided in my heart made me unique. As I grew to appreciate myself, I realized that I was a hidden gem, a treasure waiting to be discovered by someone who was truly deserving of my love.

As my confidence and self-love grew, I noticed a shift in my interactions with men. I no longer sought their approval or validation, for I had found it within myself. I knew that I was a precious gem, and any man would be blessed to have me in his life.

Eventually, I knew I would find someone who saw the beauty and value in me that I had learned to see in myself. One who would appreciate my love, compassion, and godliness. Together, we would build a relationship founded on mutual respect, admiration, and genuine affection.

In the end, being overlooked by men turned out to be a blessing in disguise. It led me on a transformative journey of self-discovery and self-love, allowing me to recognize my true worth comes from God and I had to embrace the beautiful person I am, both inside and out. Now, I stand strong in the knowledge of who I am and whose I am, a treasure that any man would be truly blessed to have.

Hidden Gem

I'm not usually the 1st option yet my personality, stature and spirit enables the beholder to see
and want to hear my voice;
A little corny or boring in some ways but intrigue has you contemplating the choice.

Those juices and berries got my skin glowing youthful
and an exotic beauty pops out from time to time if I may be truthful.

Liked that skipped track you realized was fire;
Intelligent, sexy, & silly with a bit of mystery to be desired.

So what do I taste like you wonder?
Well it's a mixture of godliness, love, exhortation, peace and support;
A tasty fulfilling meal with value and purpose that could never abort.

What could be better than what tastes good and provides nutrition and value?
yet "image", "status" or even fear forces you to have no clue.

Blinded by society or the ways you say you "used to be";
The queen you seek is right before your eyes yet you cannot see.

More than a dime since pressure has processed this diamond
and it's only a matter of time before you see its shine.

I just pray it won't be too late...

SENSE OF TASTE

Sweet yet savory, smokey memories of the smoothness on my taste buds as they heighten to Mt. Everest with no rest bursting sensations on overload.
Preserving the saltiness that jolts these flavors of love.

The sense of life sustained in one mouthful is like filling the gas tank ready to go on an extended road trip yet trippin off the chocolate taste melting and coating as it envelopes my body.

See...I need to taste every bite of you with these 2-4,000 buds that send flavors to my rooftop while there's a party going on.

Cool and hot simultaneously stimulating me as I toy with all the nooks and crannies that make up every bit of this bliss.
I don't ever want to run out of the fuel you fill me with,
so I will swallow you with necessity and digest you until all the right nutrients energize me to do it all over again.

Sense of Taste

Now get your minds out of the gutter because this was about my favorite candy bar lol. I'm not surprised though...I remember the day I was given this writing prompt about the sense of taste. It made me chuckle, as I decided to have a little fun with it by choosing to write about eating a Mr. Goodbar. My imagination soared, and I crafted this poem that I thought would evoke the simple pleasure of indulging in a delicious chocolate treat.

As I shared my poem with others, I was amused to find that people seemed to interpret it with more sensual intent, as if it were describing a sexual encounter. Their reactions surprised me, at first, and I couldn't help but smile as I observed their raised eyebrows and curious glances as I read out loud. It was fascinating to see how my words, intended to depict a sensory experience of savoring chocolate, had taken on an entirely different meaning in the minds of my audience.

The experience taught me a valuable lesson about the power of language and the way our words can be shaped by the perceptions and experiences of others. It reminded me that, as a writer, I have the ability to evoke a vast range of emotions and interpretations through my work. And sometimes, even the most innocent of writing prompts can lead to unexpected and entertaining results.

As dragonflies do bring deep meanings to the surface, I embraced the various interpretations of my poem, enjoying the playful and sensual undertones that emerged from my exploration of taste. It was a reminder that art, like life, can be full of surprises and that the simple act of eating a Mr. Goodbar could inspire so much more than I could have imagined.

AMOUR PROPRE

Good morning beautiful soul. It's the dawn of not only a new day but a new year. It's January, the 1st month of the rest of the calendar so I appreciate how you try to set the tone. Keep in mind, it's cold and gets dark early but that makes it better to hibernate. Take the time to rest and fill up because you're such a good giver and exhorter that you need time to rest, rejuvenate, and restore. The cold only chilled out the parts that didn't serve you last year. Those setbacks, health challenges, lack of love from others, the loss in your life, the uncertainty and all of the things that felt cold and/or tried to make you cold and bitter, even the coldness you dished out of ignorance, fear and/or pain, cannot remove the love gifted in you. Remember the warrior you are and don't despise the lost battles because there's beauty in your scars as they display the strength God that was put inside of you as you continue to be his walking testimony...

Good morning sweetie, love is in the air and I admire your patience as you wait for the love you so freely give. I know you get frustrated sometimes in the lonely waves and beat yourself up for the times you settled for the f-boys, non-committals and the emotionally unavailable hoping one would give you the love you ache for sometimes, but you have matured to be a faithful woman of God. Even in your temporary moments of weakness, you allow God to cleanse and strengthen you to wholeness. You now appreciate February for fun with friends and family, for you and your heart of gold that continues to shine, coat and touch every soul it encounters with your bright smile of love, kindness and gentleness...

(Sing Happy birthday in Jamaican patois) It's your birth month baby girl, ayeee...ayeee...ayeee (accented). This is the time where you reflect on who you are, where you've been, and where you want to go. Try not to get lost in where you think you are or should be going and embrace the process of being.
Did I tell you, you look good girlfriend?
Your outer beauty is radiating the love of God inside of you but I know sometimes you feel lost, empty and insecure.
It is in those moments I need you to truly remember that you are the apple of God's eye so that He keeps you in the palm of His hand.

You are valued and appreciated even though you may not feel it.
Don't get stuck in your transitions as you should recall how God has brought you from glory to glory to glory.
Continue to be his blank canvas to make His masterpiece out of your life.
I love how each year you grow in grace and wisdom. You're learning to love yourself more and guarding your heart better as you continue to love on others.
I'm so freaking proud of you girl. I'm proud of how you persevere through adversity and you are learning to take every pain and turn it into a purpose for God's glory.

Even when you're down you still manage to look up until you can get strength to get up and it's done with such grace.
It's admirable because everybody can't do that. The inner conflicts that you still struggle with won't be an issue when you let go of your ideals and ideas and really seek the mysteries of God.
Those things will start to naturally flow as the Spirit guides you to greatness. His mercy is truly upon you.

Now life has changed so you cannot travel the world like you want or even escape in the world like you used to, so you're learning to make your inner world more peaceful as you clothe in God's joy, let your brain rest, let your body be still and give it the love and care it needs from candle lit bubble baths, dressing up in your favorite perfume, pampering yourself, seeing the sights when you can, or being the creative artist that you are.

Yooooo Your visions are coming to pass and your boys are growing so nicely despite life's roller coaster ride. That is something to rejoice in. You have truly learned to embrace the beauty of the world in life. You got it going on girl...
You're an old soul with new swag and at almost 45, you're doing damn ting gal. Keep growing, keep glowing and keep embracing the beauty of life.
I am so glad you are learning to love all of you...

Hey love, I know it's probably raining in your life right now as April tends to be a stormy time of the year but I promise if you weather the storms by holding on, staying rooted and grounded in Christ along with faith and hope knowing those May flowers are just around the corner, you can get through the days of just surviving. Remember there are principles and seasons of planting and watering, sowing and reaping. God is your potter and sometimes you are being molded so expect the uncomfortable as pressure is applied. Surrender your mind, will and emotions because you're probably exhausted by the freight trains that keep crashing at your door anyway. The storms won't last forever though. Take it one day at a time until change comes. It'll be ok baby girl. You didn't make it 44 years just by sunshine. But you sure found a way to ride those rainbows...

Wake up beautiful...you made it through the stormy valleys so now it's time to enjoy the flowers that May brings. Smile because you're blooming baby. All that burying, darkness, coldness, stretching and purging brought you to the sweet savor we see in you today. Although watering and pruning will be necessary to keep you vital and growing, you are truly shining marigold so enjoy the rest of the Spring. Try to keep those in your space that truly want to be planted with you for they value the nutrients you nourish with and bring and not those that just want to admire and pick you for your intrigue & beauty...

It's your thriving season honey. You get to shed your coverings and enjoy the warmth of the sun whether on the roadways or within the beach waves. June welcomes you to truly shine your brightest and be one with nature as you enjoy the healing salt waters surrounding your pores as you definitely are a fish in water. Even Summer rain is sentimental to you as you have graduated and passed your lessons to go to the next level. You are elevating with radiance, my God you are stunning. Your energy is as electrifying as it is edifying. That fire and pressure got you shining clear and bright like the flawless diamond you are so shine on these sunny days...

You are at your peak in the blazing long days of July. Be careful you don't shed too much trying to stay cool or be cool. Stay clothed with the wings of God because the warm days make you feel free and your heat draws all kinds of energies. Even in your prosperity of purpose be careful not to get knocked off your high horse getting caught up in you...

You are wrapping up some of the brightest days as August precursors the change of Fall. Continue to cherish the last of where your melanin can roam free and gets kissed by the sun's rays. Make sure you protect yourself with the full armor of God because you can definitely burn these days. Enjoy riding the waves and make sure you take the time to be still at shore to hear them soothe you at night as they whisk back and forth washing the sand between your toes...

The last quarter of the year is upon us beautiful and it's time to grind as the warm breezy season served you well. Change is here for September so keep in mind things fall and die this season as the good long sunny days begin to shift to cooler nights. Bundle up and brace yourself as you watch the beauty fade....

I know you're scared baby girl. You lost more than you expected to that last go round but it will be ok. There are still some sweet moments and nice days ahead even though the fear of uncertainty has you on edge during this spooky time of October. You're being tricked at every stop and stretched on every side which prevents you from seeing the light at the end of the tunnel sometimes. So I'm asking you to just hold on love, I promise you clarity awaits and there is still a spark to this luminary...

Whew that was a tough one gorgeous but you persevered and made it through to November, a season of thanksgiving. You are so grateful for life, health, strength, the loved ones in your circle, the smell of warm cinnamon apples, laughter and full bellies, the crackling of fire logs, and spoils we acquired along the journey as we share memories of togetherness. It's been a fruitful year despite the pruning and you love sharing it with those around you...

Well my dear I will close out this labor of love to you as I have watched you come full circle. You are aware that endings are continuations of new beginnings, and death brings new life as December is a time for spiritual birth, magic and sparkle. Miracles, signs and wonders have pointed to the here and now. The new carols in your heart are illuminating as you have embodied the Gift that keeps on giving. You have evolved to be a bright light of hope as you fly across dragon's lairs depositing truth, harmony, unity, strength and love. You are an amazing woman and I am so blessed to have been on this journey with you. I love you so much boo!

Know that I'll be praying for the future you. Thank you for learning to love you more than another ever could on this earth. You truly are a Gift from God. Although it took you your lifetime to get to this position, it seems like you are just beginning the ride. I pray she continues to be clothed in joy, bathed in peace, in God's presence, living a productive life...blessed, whole and healed!

Amour Propre

Amour propre, or self-love, has been a guiding force in my life, teaching me valuable lessons about growth, self-awareness, and personal development. Through this journey of embracing self-love, I began to see my life as a series of lessons broken down into months and seasons.

In the winter months, I learned about resilience and strength. The cold and darkness mirrored the challenges I faced, teaching me to persevere and find warmth, within myself, through God. These months were a time of reflection and introspection, allowing me to assess my progress and set goals for the year ahead.

As spring arrived, it brought renewal and growth. I blossomed with the flowers, embracing new opportunities and experiences that came my way. I learned the importance of adapting and being open to change, understanding that change and transformation are a natural part of life.

Summer months were filled with warmth, joy, and a sense of abundance. It was during this season that I truly began to appreciate the beauty of self-love and the freedom it granted me. I learned to let go of self-doubt and limiting beliefs, basking in the sunlight of self-acceptance and confidence.

With the arrival of autumn, I was reminded of the impermanence of life and the importance of letting go. Just as the leaves fall from the trees, I allowed old habits, thoughts, and relationships that no longer served me to fall away. This season taught me the value of releasing what no longer served me, my purpose or my destiny and making space for new growth and opportunities.

Through the journey of amour propre, I came to understand that each month and season brought its own unique lessons and opportunities for growth and awareness. By embracing self-love, I was able to see the beauty and wisdom inherent in each phase of my life. This perspective allowed me to appreciate the ever-changing nature of my existence and the infinite potential that lies within me.

Today, I continue to walk this path of self-discovery and self-love, always seeking to learn and grow with each passing month and season. It is through amour propre that I have found a deeper understanding and appreciation for the journey of my life and the person I am becoming.

SET ME FREE

The day my house caught fire, my world was turned upside down. As I stood there, watching the flames consume everything I held dear, a wave of frustration and despair washed over me. I felt trapped, suffocated by the sudden loss and the weight of the challenges that lay ahead for me and my sons. In that moment, I longed to be set free from the pain and the pressures of life.

As a believer in Jesus Christ, I knew that I was no stranger to spiritual warfare. The battles I face in my everyday life are a testament to the struggle between light and darkness, a constant reminder of the forces that seek to pull me away from my faith, purpose and destiny. As I stood amidst the ashes of my home, I couldn't help but draw a parallel between the physical devastation before me and the spiritual battles I fight on a daily basis.

I began to realize that, much like the fire that had ravaged my home, the pressures of life and spiritual warfare had the potential to consume me if I allowed them to. I knew that I needed to find a way to break free from the constraints of my circumstances, to rise above the trials and tribulations that threatened to keep me bound.

In my search for freedom, I turned to my faith. I leaned on the teachings of Jesus Christ and the promise of redemption, deliverance, and restoration that He offers. As I prayed and sought solace in His word, I found the strength and courage I needed to face the challenges that lay before me and my children.

Slowly, we began to rebuild our lives, brick by brick, drawing on our faith, family and friends as a source of help, inspiration and resilience. I learned to embrace the concept of spiritual warfare as an opportunity for growth, using my struggles to deepen my relationship with God and fortify my resolve to follow His path.

Today, I stand as a testament to the power of faith and the freedom that can be found through a relationship with Jesus Christ. Though the pressures of life and spiritual warfare may continue to confront me, I am no longer bound by them. I am set free, ready to face whatever challenges come my way, with the knowledge that my Savior walks beside me every step of the way. Through seeking God first, I am able to gain the knowledge and wisdom necessary to navigate through the valleys of life and the tools to fight the enemy as the victor and overcomer I am.

Set Me Free

Walking through the valley yet I dare not fear;
Flames are turned up but I'm sure the end is near.

Refined by the fire but no smell of smoke;
Restoring all that was lost and fixing all that's broke.

Dragonflies all around to guide you along the way;
Destiny being fulfilled, purpose is its pay.

Ready for a new wave to whisk me out to sea;
Not even looking like what I've been through
since I'm walking as His living testimony.

Now watch the Patois cause

I'm ere to warn di wolf an seize di likkle fox;
Spiritual war turned natural to reset di equinox .

Territory for His Glory claiming every spoil dats due
Local turned global increased from heat,
sheepdogs warn di crew.

Now back to basics gird up for overtaking is allowed;
Harvesting all I sowed from then til now.

Tongues of fire in a language for who knows;
As many are called but only few He chose.

Wisdom shining for days like an infinite sunray;
Drawing through eyes to the soul with a smile of comfort for days.

Love manifested, enveloped to cover the multitude;
Leading the hopeless and lost to light will be my forever mood.

Grace and mercy favor my being whether I'm high or I'm low;
Uptown gyal foreva but in pilgrimage I must go.

Some plant, some water, increase in season and time;
So eat these cures I'm dishing through every verse and line...

IN THE WAITING

I remember the moment I met my husband prophetically, a vision so vivid and powerful that it felt as if destiny itself had reached out to me. The connection we shared was unlike anything I had ever experienced, transcending the boundaries of the physical world and touching the deepest corners of my soul. As I looked into his eyes, I knew that our union was meant to be ordained by a higher power to bring about incredible spiritual and emotional growth for both of us. God gave me a glimpse of my future.

Now, I find myself waiting with bated breath for reality to catch up with destiny, eager for the day when our paths will finally cross and intertwine as we will come together as one. I imagine the profound impact our union will have on our lives and on those around us, as we take our first steps into a future filled with love, joy, and divine purpose.

As I patiently wait, I continue to nurture and develop my own spiritual journey, preparing my heart and soul for the incredible adventure that awaits us. I know that the love we will share will be a catalyst for growth and transformation, a powerful force that will propel us to new heights in our spiritual and emotional development as well as to be a beacon of light and hope to others.

I anticipate the day when we will stand side by side, hand in hand, ready to face whatever challenges life may bring our way. Together, we will be a testament to the power of love and faith to conquer even the most insurmountable obstacles. Our love will be a force to be reckoned with, a bond that will transcend the limitations of the physical world and inspire those who witness it.

As I continue to wait for the unveiling of time and purpose, I find solace in the knowledge that our love is divinely guided and that our paths will cross when the time is right. And when that moment arrives, I will embrace it with open arms, ready to embark on the incredible journey that awaits us as we come together as husband and wife, united in love and purpose for eternity.

In the Waiting

An oracle once said for every prophetic word, there is an engineering work to do;
So Lord, I ask that you send the Eleazars to seam the coordinates that pixelate a picture of our lives like glue.

The Ruth in me connected to the Boaz in you
For I gleaned in your spiritual field of knowledge, wisdom and prophecy proved true.

Yet this wasn't a Cinderella story with Prince Charming to the rescue;
This was more like Hercules equipping for war with a common goal, Tangled by purpose, with shattering of emotions where sometimes bliss turned blue...

Humanity living under divinity almost caused the blessing to be missed;
Where misjudgment, fear and stubbornness tried to seal fate with a death kiss...

But like the melanated version of Princess and the Frog...life and dreams shifted roles;
where different paths merged hearts and goals
so that even when the beauty became the beast,
she was restored whole...

Prepped for union, bearing the fragrance of God,
This rose of Sharon is spirit filled, well versed for worship where the Prophetic and the Intercessor can become two peas in a pod.

Destiny can now align its path where two can become one;
for life has just begun in the eyes of eternity because prayers and intercession have won.

MEANT
TO BE

Sometimes we have to speak things as though they were. Here's a prophetic scenario about my future husband...

From the moment I laid eyes on you, I knew that something extraordinary was about to unfold. Our connection was undeniable, a force that seemed to transcend time and space. It was as if our souls had finally found their way back to one another, destined to merge and become one for eternity. And as we began our journey together, I realized that you and I were truly Kingdom mates, brought together for a purpose greater than ourselves.

Our love story is one for the ages, a tale of two hearts that found solace and strength in one another amidst the chaos of the world. Together, we discovered the beauty of selfless love, the kind of love that seeks to uplift and inspire, to nurture and protect. And as our love grew, so did our faith, our shared belief in Jesus Christ, and the evidence of the Holy Spirit guiding our steps and blessing our union.

In your arms, I found my sanctuary, a place where I could be vulnerable and true, where I could share my deepest fears and my greatest dreams. You became my rock and my refuge, the one who stood by my side through the storms and the sunshine, always there to hold my hand and wipe away my tears. And in return, I pledged my heart and my soul to you, vowing to love, honor, and cherish you for all the days of my life.

As we stand here today, surrounded by our loved ones, I am filled with a sense of awe and gratitude for the incredible journey we have embarked upon together. Our love is a testament to the power of faith and the beauty of destiny, a shining example of what it means to be true Kingdom mates. And as we prepare to take this next step in our journey, I promise to love you with every fiber of my being, to stand by your side through thick and thin, and to be the partner you deserve in this life and beyond.

In the presence of God and our loved ones, I vow to cherish our love and nurture our spiritual growth, as we embark on this journey hand in hand, heart to heart. Together, we will face the world and conquer the challenges that lie ahead, united in love, faith, and purpose. For you are my one true love, my Kingdom mate, and I am eternally grateful that our paths have crossed and our hearts have become one.

This is our love story, and as we stand here today, I am certain that it is only the beginning of a lifetime of joy, laughter, and endless adventures. For we are meant to be, our souls intertwined for a time such as now, and I cannot imagine a more perfect partner to share this incredible journey with.

Meant To Be

I'm amazed that all roads lead to you;
How God orchestrated our colliding worlds as only He foreknew.

I almost gave up that true love could exist;
From mistakes and poor choices, and life's hand of turns and twists.

A kingdom mate is not connected from this earth;
But from a realm, at the throne, given a purpose before birth.

There is a language through the spirit penetrating through the heart;
An understanding beyond thoughts and words,
much deeper than our physical parts.

I'm grateful for your generosity of the spoils in your field;
Your covering, protection and guidance as I continue to yield.

Yet nothing is to you, as you are God's vessel and link;
To help disciple His people and lead those to the everlasting Drink.

Sometimes I wonder if you are even real;
God's angel on earth thus my heart did steal.

Not perfect but perfected as God's surrendered servant;
For you are Christ's representative, Walking in truth of the Spirit with great fervence.

It IS true that God will give you more than what you could imagine or hope for;
I'm so thankful for our eternal yes,
As I am in anticipation, expectancy and excitement for what's in store...

THE ASSIGNMENT

It was during a time of deep spiritual growth and exploration that I found myself partnered with a remarkable individual on a ministry assignment. Our connection was not immediate or intense, but we seemed to complement one another perfectly every time we connected. Our shared passion for the ministry and our mutual faith in Jesus Christ made us a formidable team, and we accomplished incredible things together.

As we continued to work side by side, I couldn't help but feel a sense of divine destiny in our partnership. I began to wonder if perhaps our connection went beyond the realm of ministry, and if we were, in fact, meant to be Kingdom life mates. I had glimpses and visions of us together reaching masses of people on and off stages. Sometimes ministering together and sometimes supporting one another. The thoughts consumed me, and I allowed my heart to become entangled in the possibility of a deeper relationship.

However, as time went on, the truth became increasingly clear. Our connection, while strong and spiritually significant, was not rooted in romantic love. I had misinterpreted the nature of our bond, mistaking our ministry partnership for a divine love connection.

The realization was painful, but it was also a valuable lesson in discernment and understanding the role of divine connections in our lives. I came to see that not every deep connection is meant to be a romantic one, and that sometimes, our purpose together is to serve a higher cause, rather than to be life partners.

I am grateful for the season I spent with my ministry assignment partner. Our journey together was a powerful and transformative experience, and the work we accomplished has left a lasting impact on us and the lives of those we served. I have learned to appreciate the beauty of divine connections in all of their forms, and to trust in the wisdom of the Holy Spirit to guide my heart and my path.

As I continue on my spiritual journey, I carry with me the lessons I learned from this experience, cherishing the memories and the growth that came from my time with this incredible individual. I am reminded that our lives are filled with divine connections, each one offering its own unique gifts and opportunities for growth and possibilities. I am grateful for the chance to have shared a part of my journey with such a remarkable person.

The Assignment

Please forgive me for fantasizing about you as I'm learning to keep things straight;
We cannot afford to abort destiny, for purpose must fulfill its fate.

I want you to get all you are designed to have and be all that you're intended to be;
No matter where you end up in life and especially when that doesn't include me.

God is healing my perspective and pasturing my heart;
He is refining me in the waiting, restoring everything as He sets me apart.

I never want to be out of order with you, I value you too much for that you see;
May we be rooted in good fertile soil, waiting patiently for our harvest, as we till the ground for God's victory.

BEAUTY
AND THE BEAST

In the tapestry of my life, I've come to know many people, each one leaving a unique imprint on my heart. However, there is one male friend who stands out, mysterious and complex, reminiscent of the character Beast from the beloved tale "Beauty and the Beast." Our friendship has been a dance of delicate steps, a constant effort to balance the closeness we share with the barriers he has built around his heart.

I've always been drawn to his enigmatic presence, sensing beneath the surface a depth of emotion and vulnerability that he's hesitant to reveal. As we've grown closer over the years, I've come to understand the reasons for his guardedness, the past experiences that have left their stain and bruised mark on his heart. Yet, despite the walls he's put up, I can't help but feel a yearning for something more between us, a longing for him to open up to the possibility of real love.

As our friendship blossoms, I find myself in the role of the patient and steadfast Beauty, seeking to coax the gentle, loving soul that I know exists within him. We've shared laughter and tears, moments of solace and joy, and with each passing day, I've felt the bond between us growing stronger. I dream of the day that he will finally let down his guard and allow himself to be truly seen, to embrace the love and connection that we both so deeply desire.

In my heart, I hold onto the belief that even the most hardened of hearts can be softened by the gentle touch of love, God's unconditional love. I am determined to be the light that guides him through his darkness, the one who shows him that it's safe to trust and to love again.

So, as we continue on this journey together, I remain hopeful and patient, steadfast in my belief that our story can have a beautiful ending. I will be there for him, as a friend and a confidante, offering my unwavering support and understanding. And perhaps, one day, my dear friend will unveil the beauty within his heart, opening himself up to the love that awaits him and transforming our friendship into something even more profound and magical.

Beauty and the Beast

I didn't know I was going to end up feeling this way. I reached for you this morning to tell you about my day but you were unavailable. Couldn't wait to tell you about my new position so we could laugh and joke about me moving on up in the world.

But dead silence on the other side of the text and no answer, just voicemail that I want to replay often since I can't hear your real voice picking up my spirits and knowing exactly what my soul needs.

I felt like my friend died but I now believe it's just the transformation process of the metamorphosis of a beautiful never ending flow like crystal blue waters with a gentle breeze.

The complement of your ideas matching dreams are turning my visions into a vivid reality;
You got me on the path of my God given destiny.

Now I want to watch your babies grow into the business dynasties that keep you ruling your kingdom;
No need to fake the funk with me.
I want to help you reign your world as well as clothe you on the days you feel like a bum.

I feel your fragile love and, as scared as I am, I want to be able to give that tin man a new heart to restore the power of love, through faith, in this lifetime.

Vulnerability like crystal stairs that have been chipped away and one wrong step shatters the whole case;
but I'm not your judge or accuser, I was only assigned to defend your heart.

The BS of history don't have to be us you see because we make this thing smooth like butter baby.
We're thick like honey, and you know I'm sweet on you.

We can slow walk this thing since you already beat the shot clock when you gave me access to the doorway to our unknown.
Temporarily shut doors if you have to but please don't ever lock me out of your life.

We've already been tested, tried and true.
A real friendship enduring times of trial and triumph as our lives paralleled and the only refuge were our perpendicular paths even if we just crossed each other's minds.

I want to sync to your frequency as you become instrumental to my melodies.
I've already seen you naked with clothes on and you see I'm still here boo;
I'm not trying to tame you beast, I just want to learn how to run wild with you...

SPIRITS

As I journey through life, I've come to understand the importance of being cautious and discerning when it comes to encounters with people and forming relationships. Spiritual connections can sometimes be deceiving, distracting, and disheartening, especially when they are not rooted in God's love or when I am not in a place of healing and wholeness.

I have learned that not every person who crosses my path is meant to play a significant role in my life, and not every connection is divinely ordained. Some encounters can lead me astray, distracting me from my purpose and causing emotional turmoil. It is crucial for me to be mindful of the spirits that accompany these connections, ensuring that they align with my faith and my walk with the Lord.

In order to navigate these relationships with wisdom and discernment, I continually seek guidance from my faith and from my Heavenly Father. Through prayer, meditation, and studying the Word, I strive to maintain a strong spiritual foundation that allows me to recognize when a connection is not aligned with my highest good or God's plan for my life.

I have also come to understand the importance of personal healing and wholeness in order to forge meaningful and healthy relationships. When I am not healed or whole, I am more vulnerable to deception and manipulation, which can lead to heartbreak and disappointment. By prioritizing my spiritual and emotional well-being, I am better equipped to discern the true nature of the connections I encounter and to make wise choices regarding the relationships I cultivate.

As I continue on my life's journey, I hold fast to the lessons I have learned and the importance of being mindful of the spirits that surround me. I trust that as I seek guidance and wisdom from the Lord, He will protect and guide me, ensuring that the relationships I form are rooted in love, truth, and divine purpose. With this faith and understanding, I am better prepared to navigate the complexities of human connection, embracing those that uplift and inspire me while remaining vigilant against those that would lead me astray.

Spirits

Before I allow you in my space, I need to know What kind of spirits are you entertaining?
Cause I've been connected to people I've never even touched and our demons had a love affair that felt like spiritual bootcamp training.

Unnecessary warfare, no discernment to see,
Opened doors, blinded by desires to fulfill the wish in me.

Some sweet, some luring, some downright captivating my moods;
Familial, serpentine and marine spirits, all venomous and crude.

Smile on your face, befriending you if they must,
Only to suck the life out of you later, robbing you of your destiny and trust.

But thank God greater is He that is within you than He that is in the world I learned,
You have to suffocate the source of entry, disconnect and let those suckers burn.

Let God be your strength in weakness, always equip yourself with the Armor of God, especially in war;
For our weapons are not carnal but mighty through God to break chains and pull down strongholds like your daily chores.

A MOTHER'S FAITH

From the very moment I began to understand the concept of Mother's Day, I knew that honoring my amazing mother would be a lifelong endeavor. It's also her birthday around this time. This year, I decided to truly express my gratitude and admiration for her by writing about the remarkable impact she has had on my life.

My mother's strength, resilience, and unwavering faith have been the guiding forces that shaped me into the woman I am today. In the face of adversity, she never faltered, and her ability to persevere through life's challenges has both inspired and motivated me. She instilled in me the courage to always stand up for what I believe in and to never give up on my dreams. Her entrepreneurial spirit and courage to leave the corporate world and step into the realms of faith starting her own counseling practice was an inspiration and good guide when God had me start my EataCure health and wellness business.

Her resilience has also been a blessing to my life. Through thick and thin, my mother's determination has taught me that one can overcome any obstacle with hard work, patience, and an indomitable spirit. She has shown me that it's possible to rise above any situation and emerge stronger, wiser, and more resilient than ever before with God's strength.

But perhaps the most profound impact my mother has had on my life is her unshakable faith in Jesus Christ, our Lord and Savior. Her steadfast belief in His love, goodness, and mercy has been the foundation upon which our family is built. Her unwavering faith has been our guiding light, illuminating the path of righteousness and leading us closer to God.

My mother has not only introduced us to Jesus Christ, but she has also nurtured our faith, fostering a relationship with God that has become the cornerstone of our lives. Her dedication to prayer, scripture reading, and worship has created an environment in which our family's spiritual growth has flourished. She has taught us the importance of prayer, reverence, and humility, demonstrating the transformative power of a life devoted to Christ.

So, as Mother's Day approaches, I am filled with gratitude for the woman who has been a friend, guide, mentor and therapist to me, and my family.

To my incredible mother, thank you for being a shining example of God's love and for providing me with the foundation upon which I have built my own life. Happy Mother's Day!

A Mother's Faith

A woman with a strong foundation of faith using style and grace;
Able to withstand the trials of life with a smile on her face.

You believe in biblical truth with the true gift of faith that keeps the enemies lies at bay;
Not relying on what you see, but what you know to be true, until God makes a way.

An adventurous soul, full of life and pizazz;
Walking God's path, being an example, in good times and standing in the bad.

Giving your children and others the ultimate gift of love;
Salvation through Christ Jesus, by the Holy Spirit, linking us back to God above.

Mom, you are the epitome of strength and I'm honored to be your seed;
I'm able to walk a path worthy of God, fulfilling purpose and destiny leaving a legacy by watching you lead.

One of my biggest supporters and exhorters, a trusted confidant and listening ear,
Healing others with your counseling calling, setting captives free and defeating fear.

Not perfect but perfected in Christ;
I'm so honored to call you not only my mother but a friend in this journey called life.

Happy Mother's Day Mom
We love you!

YOU SAY

You say I'm pretty but what happens when the outer beauty fades.

Will you love the inner parts of me, my insecurities or stand by me facing
the consequences from poor choices I made.

I've had a crown of thorns and gratefully
a crown of gold.
It's only by His grace that I never grew cold.

You say you want to know me
but are you ready to dive into the depths of sea
where waves whisk you to the deep
and the only breath you breathe... is the depth of me???

A sacrificial love that enables you to be free
Yet I can't help to wonder if the same love will ever compliment me...

You Say

There he was, standing in front of me, showering me with the sweetest words and heartfelt compliments. He expressed his desire to be with me, and it was difficult to not be swept away by his charm and sincerity. Despite the warmth and affection I felt in that moment, I couldn't help but wonder if he truly understood all that I was – the good and the bad.

As we stood there, I took a deep breath and decided to challenge him. With a mixture of vulnerability and courage, I asked, "Would you still want to be with me if you knew all my flaws and mistakes? Can you accept me for who I am, with all my imperfections?"

He looked into my eyes, and for a moment, I saw a flicker of uncertainty. But then, he took my hands and said, "I know you're not perfect, and neither am I but we are perfected in Christ. We all have our flaws and make mistakes; it's part of being human. That's why we need God. I'm not looking for a faultless partner, but someone who is willing to grow and learn with me. As long as we're honest with each other and communicate openly, I believe we can overcome any obstacle."

His words resonated with me, but I needed to know more. I needed to know if the love I had to offer would be appreciated and reciprocated, so I asked, "Will the love I give be complemented? Can we support each other, care for each other, and create a nurturing relationship?"

He smiled and replied, "I believe love is not just about what we can take from each other, but also what we can give. I want to be there for you, to support you, and to make you feel loved and appreciated. And in return, I hope that you'll do the same for me. I believe that together, our love can grow stronger and more beautiful each day."

His response warmed my heart and reassured me that he was willing to embrace both the beauty and complexity of our relationship. As we stood there, hands entwined, I felt a profound sense of hope and excitement for the journey that lay ahead. Together, we would embark on a path filled with love, understanding, and growth, ready to face the challenges and embrace the joys that life would bring our way.

BLUE DIAMOND

Blue Diamond status;
Understanding there's not too many of us.

Pressured beyond the norm;
Trusted to weather every storm.

The rarity identifies its clarity;
Not the environment of its process you see.

Colored by its ability to absorb in the deepest dark places;
Making its shine so much greater when it reaches the surface.

420 miles below the ocean's floor sweep;
Most of you aren't equipped to handle the hot water you steep.

Sustained in life's waves, ebbs and flows;
Knowing what is necessary to continue to grow.

Called and cherished by a chosen few;
Now being sent for, as your table has been waiting for you.

Blue Diamond

I remember my pastor teaching about blue diamonds one day and I was so intrigued because I never heard of one. So I researched to see for myself. As I gazed upon the exquisite blue diamond, I couldn't help but marvel at its striking beauty and rarity. The intricate process that transformed it from a rough stone into a breathtaking gemstone resonated deeply with me, as I saw parallels between its journey and my own.

Just like the blue diamond, I too have been formed under immense pressure and heat. Life's challenges have shaped me, molding me into the unique person I am today. Each experience, whether positive or negative, has left an indelible mark, akin to the inclusions and imperfections that contribute to the diamond's character.

The exquisite blue hue, a result of trace elements of boron, reminded me of my own distinct qualities. For those that don't know, I'm a scientist so this was also a teachable moment for me. My individuality, my passions, and my quirks are the trace elements that make me who I am, setting me apart from the rest. The blue diamond's captivating color is rare and valuable, and I too embrace my own rarity, understanding that my uniqueness is my strength.

It takes a skilled craftsman to bring out the true brilliance of a blue diamond, cutting and polishing it to perfection, revealing its true potential. Similarly, the people who have entered my life have played a vital role in shaping me, helping me grow and evolve. They've polished away my rough edges, revealing the best version of myself.

As I contemplated the blue diamond's journey, I felt a deep appreciation for my own path. Its rarity and the process it went through to become a mesmerizing gemstone are a reminder of my own uniqueness and the experiences that have shaped me. Just like the blue diamond, I am a rare and priceless treasure in and to this world, and I am proud of the person I have become.

THE POWER
WITHIN ME

As a child of God, I have come to understand the immense power that resides within me. This divine power enables me not only to stand firm against the forces of darkness but also to help others in their battles against spiritual warfare. I have come to realize that my faith and trust in the Lord equips me to face the powers, principalities, and wickedness that often manifest in high places.

Ephesians 6:12 states, "For our struggle is not against flesh and blood, but against the rulers, against the authorities, against the powers of this dark world and against the spiritual forces of evil in the heavenly realms." This verse illuminates the nature of the battles I face daily, reminding me that as a believer, I am called to engage in spiritual warfare.

Through the power of prayer, praise and worship, I have been able to overcome challenges and obstacles that once seemed insurmountable. By putting on the full armor of God, I have been able to stand firm in my faith, resisting the devil and his schemes. The helmet of salvation, the breastplate of righteousness, the belt of truth, the shield of faith, the shoes of the gospel of peace, and the sword of the Spirit – these are the weapons that empower me to prevail against the forces of darkness.

As I walk in victory, I have discovered that my triumphs in spiritual warfare can also be a source of blessing and freedom for others. Through my testimony, I can inspire and encourage others to stand strong in their faith, equipping them to fight their own battles against the enemy. By sharing my experiences and the power of God's Word, I can help others find the strength they need to overcome adversity and resist temptation. For the Bible says, "we overcome by the blood of the Lamb and the word of our testimony." (Revelation 12:11)

Moreover, as I intercede for others in prayer, I am able to help them break free from the chains of spiritual bondage. My petitions before the Lord can bring about deliverance, healing, and restoration in the lives of those who are ensnared by the enemy. By standing in the gap for them, I can be a conduit of God's grace and mercy, empowering them to experience victory over the powers, principalities, and wickedness that seek to oppress them.

As a child of God, I am called to engage in spiritual warfare, both for my own sake and for the sake of others. Through the power and authority that I have been granted in Christ, I can overcome the forces of darkness, stand firm in my faith, and be a source of blessing and freedom for those who are entangled in spiritual battles. This is my divine mission and my privilege as a believer, and I am grateful for the opportunity to serve the Lord in this way. Read this declaration with me.

The Power Within Me

As I was listening to destiny I almost got ran off the road;
Yet Faith shielded me back to the narrow path because it's in my genetic code.

There's a purpose in me....
A divine purpose to set the captives free;
Where every snake, witch and evil force must flee,
Because the power of Jesus Christ resides in me.

I speak to the little child whose voice got muffled;
To the fear that grips you and confusion that keeps you shuffled.

Say there's strength in me....
A divine purpose to set the captives free;
Where every snake, witch and evil force must flee,
Because the power of Jesus Christ resides in me.

A power to mobilize the paralyzed,
Motion to the stuck;
Restoration to the fallen,
Healing from heaven not luck.

Believe there's power in me...
A divine purpose to set the captives free;
Where every snake, witch and evil force must flee,
Because the power of Christ resides in me.

To every doubter, hater and naysayer,
The false friends and cheating players;
You are all part of God's plan to get the expected end;
Never broken even when battered or on the bend.

Know there's a destiny in me....
A divine purpose to set the captives free;
Where every snake, witch and evil force must flee,
Because the power of Christ resides in me.

To speak life not death...edify and not bury,

To honor God with my being and have a purified heart where the Holy Spirit dwells so there's no need to worry;
From a tent dweller to a Kingdom builder,
walking in dignity and grace;
Not to be haughty or prideful for I am forever seeking His face.

Understand there's a miracle in me...
A divine purpose to set the captives free
Where every snake, witch and evil force must flee
Because the power of Christ resides in me.

There's Power in Me!

THE EYES OF DECEPTION BEFORE TIME

There was a time when I was deceived into believing that I had found my soulmate, a man who seemed to be everything I had ever dreamed of. Our connection was great, almost divine, and it seemed as though our familiar spirits had united us in a holy and righteous bond. Little did I know that this relationship was not of God and that I had been led astray by the cunning deception of the enemy.

In the beginning, everything felt perfect. Our conversations flowed effortlessly, our interests aligned, and our spiritual beliefs appeared to be in harmony. I was convinced that this was a blessing from God, and I was grateful for companionship that I believed He had sent my way. Man was blindsided.

As time went on, however, subtle signs began to emerge, indicating that this relationship was not what it seemed. Our spiritual discussions started to reveal differences in our beliefs that I had not initially noticed. I noticed he was compromising his values and was drifting further away from the principles that had once guided his life.

Despite the growing uneasiness in my heart, I was reluctant to let go of this relationship. The connection we shared felt so powerful, it was like we could read each other's minds and speak to each other telepathically. I was afraid of losing what I thought was a divine gift. It was then that I realized that our familiar spirits had deceived me into believing that this relationship was holy and righteous, when in reality, it was a snare designed to pull me away from God's will for my life.

In my despair, I turned to God, seeking His guidance and wisdom. Through prayer and reflection, I came to understand that the connection I had experienced was not of God, but rather a deceptive ploy of the enemy. I realized that I had allowed myself to be misled by my desires, blinded to the truth that was right in front of me. The crazy thing was, we never even met in person. I was deceived by intellect and spiritual gifts that are given without repentance, meaning you can operate in spiritual gifts whether you are walking God's righteous path or not.

With the heaviest heart I ever had, I made the difficult decision to end the connection, trusting that God had a better plan for my life. I hurt like never before and I couldn't understand why because we were not in a relationship and we never touched each other in person let alone be physically intimate. We weren't even that close of friends for me to feel so devastated. I remember literally feeling like I was dying on the inside one night that even the person praying for me that night was concerned. Weeping truly endured for a night yet I was grateful for the joy that came in the morning. As I let go of the false sense of security that the familiar spirits had offered, I felt a renewed sense of clarity and purpose. I committed myself to seeking God's will in all aspects of my life, especially when it came to matters of the heart.

The Bible says in Proverbs 4:23 to "Above all else, guard your heart, for everything you do flows from it." The Lord means for us to guard our hearts by filtering our emotions, desires, thoughts, and responses through his

Word so that when things arise, his Word trumps whatever it is. Our souls now become protected with the truth of the Word.

In retrospect, I understand that the enemy will use any means necessary to deceive us and lead us away from God's purpose. The experience taught me the importance of discerning the true nature of man and relationships by seeking God's guidance in all things. You shall know them by their fruit...allow time to reveal the fruit in its season before investing or committing mind, body and spirit. This goes for any and everything as well as everyone. I now know that only by aligning myself with God's will that I can find true happiness and fulfillment in life, free from the snares of deception.

Before Time

Sometimes I wonder if you are just a figment of my imagination, as your smile stays on repeat in my mind;
the way I feel like you go to bat for me, even in stern teaching,
but especially when you're kind.

I must've bumped my head seeing our future before my eyes;
The way we are connected from eternity to present,
I can't allow my heart to ever say goodbye.

The way you comment on my convos like you're a fly on my wall;
The way you understand my unspoken words beyond emotions especially since I answered God's call.

You asked how did I come to know you as you were unaware I was there,
however our virtual encounter proved our connected presence as laughs, discussion and energy exploded in the
air.

Maybe it's me...Maybe the wish got the best of me.
I don't mind waiting, I just want some assurity that what I see I know is true;
that forever was meant to be for me and you.

I apologize for not exhibiting the Spirit's fruits as impatience's desire gets flicked;
but don't you know that hope deferred makes the heart sick?
I just want the truth because you are like a habit that I can't kick.

And I don't want a good time for a short time for longevity has to be this recipe;
just waiting on some clarity before this becomes the death of me.

I admit, I got it bad for you babe for I just want to see you face to face,
to experience love manifested through God's Grace;
For you to be ready to experience me in time and space as we finish life's race.

The Eyes of Deception

I didn't even know our demons could play with each other like that;
I guess that's how soul ties start and illusions become deluded fantasies turned whack.

Believing we were connected by spirit and mind;
Before ever thinking of bodily touches feeling divine.

Oh we were connected alright but only by wishes and desires not surrendered by God;
where the enemy got a foothold yoking us in deception pods.

See... like spirits draw one another by the scent of bloodhounds;
then they fortify their watchmen and entourage to keep one another bound.

You feel like it's from heaven not knowing you willingly gave hell the keys;
Access to your being through your mind not surrendered on your knees.

Supplanters and wolves all around dressed up like sheep;
Infiltrating through whatever you didn't give God to sweep.

Pride wouldn't let me admit the weakness of not turning over every gift, talent, thought, action, or concern;
so now the enemy has a foothold that became his gateway for me to burn.

FALSE PRETENSES

I never thought I would find myself in a relationship where deception and manipulation would play such a significant role. At first, everything seemed perfect. My partner was attentive, charming, and appeared genuinely committed to our relationship. As time went by, however, I began to realize that the person I wanted to fall in love with was not who they claimed to be.

Subtle inconsistencies in their stories and behavior gradually revealed themselves, making me question the authenticity of our connection. Initially, I dismissed my concerns, fearing that I was being overly critical or paranoid. However, as the inconsistencies multiplied, I could no longer ignore the growing sense of unease that was apparent.

When I finally confronted my partner, seeking clarity and honesty, the truth came out. Their carefully constructed image began to crumble, as I learned that I had been deceived and manipulated. The person I thought I knew had been wearing a mask, concealing their true nature and intentions.

I was devastated, feeling betrayed and foolish for having fallen for such deceit. As I tried to make sense of the situation, I questioned my judgment and wondered if I could ever trust myself or anyone else again. However, I knew that allowing this experience to break me was not an option. I had to find a way to heal and rebuild my confidence.

I started the healing process by seeking God. I realized that while I couldn't control the actions of others, I could take responsibility for my own well-being and growth.

As I worked through the pain and betrayal, I gradually began to regain my sense of self and trust in my judgment. I learned to be more discerning and to trust my intuition when something felt off. I vowed never to let myself be deceived by false pretenses and manipulation again.

In the end, this painful experience taught me the importance of vigilance and trusting my instincts in relationships. While the deception and manipulation were difficult to endure, the lessons learned have made me stronger and more resilient. Today, I approach relationships with newfound wisdom and a commitment to nurturing genuine connections based on trust, honesty, and authenticity.

False Pretenses

It wasn't love it was obsession;
Disguised in passion but really was control and possession.

Manipulation masked with a smile of kindness;
Desires of the flesh will have you walking in total blindness.

In matters of the heart, always falling for the wish;
Must be purified by God's fire to get rid of that ish!

In the wilderness journey, consecration weakens the soul;
Not to punish but to purify, so your will can fold.

There's always casualties in war so you will lose what you hoped to gain;
But I promise dying to self will NOT be in vain.

The record of wrong that stood against me is nailed to the cross;
In redemption, I am encouraged, I will gain more than what was lost.

You will have what you need and want in due season;
But God has to stay the 1st source and reason.

Resisting the enemy so he can flee;
Being honest that the enemy...sometimes is me...

BLACK DON'T
CRACK

Black don't crack unless you starve it with lack.
Juices and berries energize not only the body but the soul;
Melanin be poppin preserving the skin from wrinkles of old.

But you can't forget to free your mind of the old wives tales;
By removing the cataracts from your eyes that blind you from scales.

Black Don't Crack

For years, I had heard the saying, "Black don't crack," and I believed it to be true. I had seen the evidence in the radiant faces of my elders, their smooth skin defying their age. However, I came to understand that this ageless beauty is not a guarantee, but rather a gift that must be nurtured and cared for. "Black don't crack unless you starve it with lack," I realized, as I began to learn the importance of taking care of both my body and my mind.

I discovered that juices and berries had the power to energize not only my body but also my soul. The vibrant colors and flavors of these natural wonders invigorated me, providing the essential nutrients needed to maintain my health and vitality. As I nourished my body from within, I could feel my melanin poppin', preserving my skin from the wrinkles of old and giving it a youthful glow.

But taking care of the body is only part of the equation. I also learned the importance of freeing my mind from the old wives' tales that had been passed down through generations. These stories, while often amusing and charming, could sometimes perpetuate limiting beliefs and misconceptions. To truly care for my mind, I needed to remove the cataracts from my eyes and strip away the scales that blinded me from the truth.

As I embarked on this journey of self-discovery and growth, I found that nourishing my body and mind was an act of self-love and respect. By embracing a holistic approach to wellness, I was able to preserve the beautiful gift of my melanin-rich skin, while also cultivating a clear and open mind.

I came to understand that "Black don't crack" is not just a catchy phrase, but a call to action. It is a reminder to nurture and honor the unique beauty and strength that lies within us, by taking care of both our bodies, our minds and our spirits. This is the key to unlocking our true potential and living our most vibrant, fulfilling lives.

DON'T AWAKEN
LOVE
BEFORE IT'S TIME

As I look toward the future, my heart swells with anticipation and excitement. I dream of the path that lies ahead, the wondrous experiences and milestones I will encounter, and the deep connections I will forge. One of the most profound desires within me is to find true love, a partnership that radiates joy, understanding, and, most importantly, aligns with God's will. However, I am mindful of the potential pitfalls of rushing into love and not allowing it to blossom organically and at the right time.

The words from Song of Solomon 8:4 resonate within me: "Do not awaken love before it so desires." This gentle reminder cautions me against forcing love to unfold before its time, as doing so may lead to heartache and disappointment. By trusting in God's divine plan and timing, I can ensure that the love I ultimately find will be anchored in His will and purpose for my life.

In my quest for love, I strive to remain patient and steadfast in my faith. I pray for guidance, asking for God's wisdom and discernment to lead me to the right person, at the right time. I am committed to cultivating my relationship with God, knowing that a strong spiritual foundation will be the cornerstone of any healthy, lasting partnership.

As I continue on my journey, I am constantly reminded that God's timing is perfect. While it may be tempting to try and control the course of my life, I must trust in His plan and be patient in my pursuit of love. By not awakening love before its time, I allow myself the opportunity to grow and prepare for the beautiful and divine union that awaits me, a love story orchestrated by God Himself.

So, with anticipation and faith, I look forward to the future, confident in the knowledge that God's will shall be done. I embrace the joy and challenges of my journey, remaining ever mindful of the importance of not awakening love before its time. And when that time finally comes, I know that my heart will be ready, my spirit aligned, and the love I find will be truly blessed by the hand of God.

Don't Awaken Love Before It's Time

I'd love nothing more than to feel your touch as sweat a go buss through each pulse and thrust;
Yet I realized I get uncomfortable when love turns to lust,
When purity of spirit changes, invoking lack of trust.

As expressively passionate as I am,
especially in its prime;
I cannot awaken love before it's time,
We are building something special to last a lifetime.

Emotional overload as our connection explodes,
needs a firm foundation or what we have will implode.

I don't want fantasies turned to nightmares or smiles to turn to bitter stares;
To crown a stage not in full bloom is a catastrophe I cannot bear.

To stir up passions with no release,
tends to embrace moments that lead to no peace.

I know it's hard, as a man shows love through the physical;
but a divine intervention ordained what is mystical.

To live through the spirit and not through the flesh,
will have this love grow naturally without distress.

I promise I'm worth the wait for I am more than a dime;
just let destiny fulfill itself and not awaken love before its time...

LESS OF A HOME

One day, as I walked down the bustling streets of the city, I saw a homeless man sitting on the sidewalk. His eyes were tired, and his clothes were worn and tattered. I didn't have any money but I did have some EataCure juice products leftover from my event so I gave him some of the sea moss juice bottles. He thanked me as I prayed it would give him the nutrients he needed as well as hell with any ailments. As I observed him, a thought struck me like a bolt of lightning: anyone could end up in his position at any time. I suddenly realized that life can be unpredictable, and circumstances can change in the blink of an eye.

This revelation led me to be more sensitive to the experiences of others and to recognize the importance of empathy and compassion. I began to understand that no one is immune to life's hardships, and it is crucial to lend a helping hand whenever possible.

I used to take my boys to help feed the homeless when they were young but I didn't realize the impact it could have had until life becomes real for you! We just thought it was the right and noble thing to do growing up in a Christian home. When life starts "lifing" as society says today, you realize it could be you. I remember almost losing my house when I got ill. Being paralyzed and bedridden for 10 years was not easy after a divorce. I no longer had a partner, career and my kids were young so they couldn't help. I had family and friends supporting but not enough to sustain my household and it took me almost 4 years before I received disability assistance. Then years later we bounced around from place to place after our house fire...BUT GOD!

From that moment on, I made an effort to support those in need and offer assistance whenever I could. To this day I'm grateful to lend a helping hand at a local organization, providing food and clothing to those who need them. In doing so, I discovered the power of human connection and the impact that even the smallest act of kindness can have on someone's life.

I learned an invaluable lesson: life can be fragile, and we must be sensitive to the experiences of others. Never judge a book by its cover. By extending our help and understanding, we can make a difference in the lives of those who need it most.

Less of a Home

I was looking for help with my hunger and thirst. Thirst for food and drink, yes, but more importantly His Word. I just needed to know I can hold onto something for where I was today as I reminisced on the time when I was that supervisor on my job...oh wait, did you think I was in this situation...my whole life? They say never judge a book by its cover but you never picked up the book for the dust and dirt deterred you from seeing the beauty of the words to my pages of life.

See I am no different from you, just circumstances often outside of our control forced me to be stuck where I lost all the things others take for granted. I went from being listened to for instruction to being avoided even when my screams come out as whispers or just facial expressions to wear because my voice is no longer heard.

I may have even picked up a habit or two to numb the pain of my unforeseen journey, as many of you do daily, longing to hear and see that God has a better plan for me.

Maybe I am that refugee that had to relocate after the storm tore up my community and never was able to get back on my feet.

I am also that divorcee that never stood a chance when the judge ordered me to go.

That downsized position was only the indicator that the company was about to be no more and even though education was supposed to offer a better chance at life, I am now outdated and irrelevant for today's times...and rents and mortgages only extend for so long.

Imagine being the head honcho until sickness grips you and strips you of all you own and know. The system only provides to the fault of its limitations and sorry is the only thing you walk away with.

Whatever happened to taking care of those that can't take care of themselves. Especially when I see the daily waste and disregard for food and clothing. There are places where a child holds on to one sandwich for dear life to feed his whole family that night.

We have the power and authority to make a difference. Encourage those going through struggles and trials in their lives as a reminder that our circumstances don't dictate who we are. Unfortunately, illness, tragedy, fire, loss of jobs, divorce, struggles with people, places and things, life's transitions and even flat out poor choices cause all of us to be in situations uncomfortable and unfair at times.

Desperation and despair set in especially with the loss of family, friends and possessions like our homes. This can be any one of us at any given time. So please help out where you can in thought, action and deed. "For we are all born with value and purpose, our lives have promise and potential as it unfolds in accordance to God's eternal plan...." (my old church proclamation)

THE WOMAN AT THE WELL

As I reflect on my life, I can't help but draw a parallel between my experiences and the story of the woman at the well in the Bible. Just like her, I found myself longing for and leaning on people, places, and things for fulfillment instead of seeking solace in God.

I was married to the ideas of approval, acceptance, and acknowledgment from others, constantly seeking validation in my relationships, career, and social circles. This insatiable desire to be accepted left me feeling empty and unfulfilled, like a well that could never be filled.

One day, as I came across the story of the woman at the well in the Bible, It touched me in a way I never read it before. The new revelation had so much significance for my life. Jesus offered her living water, a source of eternal fulfillment that could quench her thirst once and for all. At that moment, I realized how I had been searching for satisfaction in all the wrong places.

I knew it was time for me to take off the clothes of insecurity, fear, and doubt that had weighed me down for so long. Just like the woman at the well, I needed to embrace the living water offered by Jesus and let it wash away my need for external validation.

I began to seek God's presence in my life, turning to Him for guidance, comfort, and strength when I felt lost, afraid, or uncertain. As I cultivated my relationship with Him, I discovered a sense of peace and fulfillment that surpassed anything the world could offer.

Now, when I am tempted to look for approval, acceptance, or acknowledgment from others, I remind myself of the woman at the well and the living water that Jesus offers. I have learned that true fulfillment can only be found in God, and it is through His love and grace that I am able to walk confidently, free from the shackles of insecurity, fear, and doubt.

The Woman at the Well

That moment you face the mirror and embrace the sting.
From longing for people, places and things.

Looking for love in all the wrong places;
when it is really God that you seek to fill your empty spaces.

See...The day I realized I was the woman at the well, thirsting and longing for people to dwell.

I had 5 husbands and even the one I was recently with was not mine
as I needed to be filled by only the one true Divine.

Married to and thirsting for acknowledgment, appreciation, and praise;
not recognizing I am the apple of His eye and His admiration goes on for days.

To drink from THIS well is a quench of your thirst for a lifetime
For you will no longer care to desire temporary things that fade with time.

To no longer depend on the undependable nature of man;
To suffer pain and heartache from disappointment and rejection for the things that only He can.

To cry your last tear for missing the mark,
knowing grace, mercy and favor cover you, especially in the dark.

I'm humbled and amazed by the vulnerability of my soul,
but trusting in His craftsmanship, that even in my complexities, I can still be bold.

I am learning to seek Him, to think like Him, move like Him, and see like Him.
But It's something that cannot be done on a whim.

I'm establishing a relationship to a covenant He made before I was born;
to be destined for a purpose before my first outfit was even worn.

Taking off the clothes of insecurity, fear and doubt;
bathing in His presence... covered in His glory...overflowing with His oil..
Now understanding what my life is truly about.

Not focusing on the things I have to do but how to be, learning to be rooted and grounded, firmly like a tree.

LAPS

I swam a lap of regret for every moment you felt like you waited in vain;
Forgive me for being so blind to your gentle heart,
For insanity's pain made me question if you were a loss or gain.

In protecting myself I hurt you as well as myself;
For it forced you into a shell as you tucked your love on the back shelf.

Oh How I long to see those dreamy eyes light up with the fuel from my sight again;
To see your smile of joy in my presence not worrying about if you should fight or defend.

If I get to chance to warm the fire and melt the ice;
Trust and believe, I would not be a fool twice.

I want to shower you with every beat of my heart;
Flowing rapidly smooth as I breathe your sweetness when we rewind back to start.

Laps

There I was, swimming in laps of regret as I realized the consequences of hiding my genuine love, affection, and attention in a past relationship. I had allowed my previous pain and uncertainty to dictate my actions, and it had cost me dearly. My partner, sensing my emotional withdrawal, had drawn back his love and openness, unsure if he could ever open up again.

My heart ached as I recalled the countless moments when I could have shown my love and vulnerability, but instead chose to keep my emotions locked away which is actually against the grain of me. I had convinced myself it was for the best, a way to protect myself from further heartache. But in doing so, I had inadvertently stifled the emotional connection we had once shared.

As I continued to swim through my sea of regret, I couldn't help but feel a deep sense of loss. I mourned for the relationship that could have been, and for the love that had once been so strong. I had allowed fear to control my actions, and now I was left to face the consequences.

Determined to make amends, I resolved to learn from my mistakes and to never let fear hold me back from expressing my true emotions again. I had to learn how to guard my heart but still show the love God placed inside of me. I understood now that hiding my feelings had only caused more pain and uncertainty for both of us.

Though I couldn't change the past, I promised myself that I would strive to be more open and vulnerable in my future relationships. I knew that the only way to truly experience love and connection was to allow myself to be seen and heard, in all of my emotional complexity.

As I emerged from my laps of regret, I carried a newfound sense of self-awareness and a commitment to never again let fear dictate my actions in love. I realized that the vulnerability I had once shied away from was the very key to nurturing deep, meaningful connections, and I vowed to embrace it wholeheartedly moving forward.

A REAL FRIEND

I want to be your friend beyond my needs and expectations;
To be your nonjudgmental zone as I step outside of myself for your situations.

A listening ear and a shoulder to cry;
A trustworthy source to protect your questioned whys.

A breath of fresh air,
an intercessor for prayer.

A joy for your pain,
your peace in life's strain.

A cheerleader in your cause,
your partner when you pause

Your strength on leaning sides,
You're constant when all else says goodbye.

A Real Friend

As I thought about the men I dealt with in my life, I realized that what I truly desired was to be a real friend to him. I understood that the foundation of a strong relationship was built on the pillars of true friendship, support, and selflessness, all centered in God.

I wanted to be the person he could lean on, confide in, and trust implicitly. I longed to create an atmosphere of openness and understanding, where we could share our hearts and minds without fear of judgment or rejection. I knew that such a connection could only be achieved by bringing God into the center of our relationship, allowing His love and grace to guide us.

With this goal in mind, I set out to cultivate a friendship rooted in selflessness and support. In my last relationship, I made an effort to truly listen to him, to understand his dreams, fears, and struggles, and to offer my encouragement and guidance whenever needed. I sought to create a safe space for us to grow together, both as individuals and as a couple.

As our friendship deepened, I found that our relationship began to flourish in new and unexpected ways. We became more attuned to each other's needs, more willing to compromise and work through challenges, and more in sync with each other's emotions. Our bond, once centered in God, grew stronger and more resilient with each passing day.

As I continued on this journey of being a real friend to the man in my life, I discovered the true meaning of love and companionship. I learned that the most profound connections are built on a foundation of trust, support, and selflessness, all of which are grounded in our shared faith. Through the ups and downs, I am grateful for the opportunity to grow together as friends, partners, and followers of God.

SOUL MUSIC SPEAKS

One day, as I was reflecting on my experiences with relationships, I decided to have some fun with a creative writing exercise. I wanted to explore the theme of love and connection through the lens of song titles, and so I began working on a play on words with this next piece entitled "Soul Music Speaks."

As I started writing, I couldn't help but feel a wave of inspiration wash over me. I began weaving together a tapestry of song titles that told the story of a love that blossomed, faced challenges, stood the test of time, but eventually ended in loss.

As I put the finishing touches on "Soul Music Speaks," I marveled at the power of music and the way it could tell the story of love and relationships so eloquently. I had woven a narrative through the melodies and lyrics of these iconic songs, and in doing so, I had discovered a new way to express the complex emotions that accompany the journey of love.

Soul Music Speaks

Waiting on that Total Eclipse of the Heart taking these NE Heartbreaks on the chin. So Lost in Emotion that I am bound for a win.

I'm loving that Brown Skin as I ride that Chocolate High. Imma Give You the Best That I Got for You Bring Me Joy in unlimited supply.

I give you Permission to act on these Wild Thoughts just make sure you catch me when I Fall For You without fear; (or 2nd gear...)
Not worrying about other people because They Gonna Talk for They Don't Know about this thing right here.

I'm ready for the Exchange because You Earned it and I will make sure you Don't Forget About Us in between thrusts because my love is Unforgettable when Sweat a go Buss.

Nothing Even Matters when I'm With You. That 24K Magic got me feeling purified after all the hell I've been through.
I'm trying to get to those 5 Steps of Eternity, taking that Stairway to Heaven feeling Lost Without You.

We were just Ordinary People Thinking Out Loud back then...now I gotta contemplate the Start Over with this Contradiction when all I wish I could do is Remember the Times You Rocked My World since we are barely on the scoreboard compared to constantly scoring that perfect 10.

You made me your Sweet Lady making lifetime promises only to bounce them checks against an empty love account and like a fox you were sly;
It's all fun and games til someone gets hurt but I'm good because the way my resilience is set up homie...please understand Big Girls Don't Cry.

I just want to know Where Are You Now because I feel like you are screaming silent Hellos from the other side after turning them gray Skies blue;
I Can't Make You Love Me so you might want to Listen before I take my Next Breath and see that I need you to Say Something because I'm Giving Up on You...

FORGIVE ME LORD

It was a dark and stormy night when the weight of my spiritual warfare finally took its toll on me. Betrayed by those I loved, my heart cried out in anguish, and I found myself questioning my faith. I felt weary and defeated, and in that moment of vulnerability, I turned to God for solace.

I asked Him for forgiveness, not only for my weariness but also for the times when I had allowed my hurt to consume me. I realized that my pain, while significant, paled in comparison to the rejection God experiences every day from the very people He created.

As I prayed, I began to see the bigger picture – how humanity has tried to become its own divinity without God as their guide. People have become lovers of themselves, thriving in corruption and casting God aside.

I thought about the countless souls who had turned away from God, seeking solace in their own self-serving pursuits. As I pondered this, I understood that my own suffering was a mere fraction of the heartache that God endures.

With this newfound perspective, I renewed my commitment to stand strong in my faith, even when faced with adversity and betrayal. I vowed to remember the sacrifices that God has made for us, through Christ Jesus, and to strive to be a source of love and light in a world that often seems consumed by darkness.

As I continued to pray, I felt a renewed sense of strength and purpose. I knew that, with God by my side, I could overcome the challenges that lay ahead. I also understood the importance of empathy and compassion in my spiritual journey, recognizing the struggles that others face and offering my support whenever possible.

I emerged from my moment of weakness with a deeper connection to God and a greater appreciation for the power of forgiveness and resilience. I knew that, through Him, I could weather any storm and emerge stronger than ever before.

Forgive Me Lord

Lord forgive me for my selfish and self centered ways;
Not wanting to bear the burden and pray these past few days.

Let it be about You Lord and not me, surrendering to your Will;
I know there are casualties in war so I'll learn to just be still.

Not leaning on my own understanding trusting the mysteries of Your heart;
Even the glimpses you show me are only in part.

But sometimes it hurts to bear the burdens of warnings
and to see betrayal in the ones you love;
I can only imagine the ripple of my small pebble compared to what you feel from above.

How humanity has tried to become divinity without You as their guide;
To be lovers of themselves, thriving in corruption casting You aside.

About the Author

DragonFly aka Marcia Marie Moore has been writing poetry since age 12. Marcia uses poetry to express her emotions of her journey through life, love and spirituality. As dragonflies bring deep meanings to light, the duality in Marcia's poems speak volumes in layers to impact any and every soul, with hope and light.

DragonFly Chronicles Vol 1 Poetry CD is available on CD Baby, itunes, and all streaming outlets. Marcia also has 3 published books on Amazon where e-versions are just 99 cents! Marcia: Poems From the Heart, Marcia: Eyes to the Soul and Marcia: Thoughts From My Mind by Marcia M. Harvey.

DragonFly has performed all over the United States with empowering favorites including Scaled, I Matter, Local Chick and I Am Not Ready. You can find Marcia's work under @dragonflymarcia on IG or links at www.eatacure.com

Set Me Free, released on all streaming platforms, is her latest single off of the upcoming DragonFly Unleashed album.

Don't forget to check out I Matter, Letter to My Sons and No More F Boys Videos on YouTube under Marcia Marie Wellness or search EataCure Wellness.

Made in the USA
Middletown, DE
10 July 2023

34480005R00059